WILLIS REED

CHARLES OAKLEY

ERNIE VANDEWEGHE

LARRY JOHNSON

BILL BRADLEY

PATRICK EWING

EARL MONROE

JERRY LUCUS

CARL BRAUN

BERNARD KING

LATRELL SPREWELL

WALT FRAZIER

CREATIVE EDUCATION

Published by Creative Education, 123 South Broad Street, Mankato, MN 56001

Creative Education is an imprint of The Creative Company.

Designed by Rita Marshall

Photos by Allsport, AP/Wide World, Rich Kane, NBA Photos

Library of Congress Cataloging-in-Publication Data

Goodman, Michael E. The history of the New York Knicks / by Michael E. Goodman.

p. cm. — (Pro basketball today)   ISBN 1-58341-107-0

1. New York Knickerbockers (Basketball team)—History—

Juvenile literature. [1. New York Knickerbockers (Basketball team)—History.

2. Basketball—History.] I. Title. II. Series.

GV885.52.N4 G65 2001   796.323'64'097471—dc21   00-047328

First Edition 9 8 7 6 5 4 3 2 1

IN 1626, A GROUP OF DUTCH SETTLERS PURCHASED A SMALL ISLAND ALONG THE MIDDLE ATLANTIC COAST AND CALLED IT

New Amsterdam. These settlers wore special knee-length pants called "knickerbockers," or "knickers" for short. Less than 40 years later, the settlement was passed along to the British, who renamed it New York. Much of the city's Dutch heritage faded over the years, but the term "Knickerbocker" stayed alive and was used to describe any resident who could trace his or her ancestry back to the original settlers.

Knickerbocker took on a new meaning in 1946, when a new professional basketball league called the Basketball Association of America

BUD PALMER

(BAA) was founded. After New York was awarded a franchise, its own-

ers needed to pick a name for the club and put several suggestions in a

The Knicks
were an
instant
success,
making the
playoffs in
their first
10 seasons. hat. Knickerbockers was the name drawn out, and the

New York Knicks were born.

{BUILT ON BRAUN} From the start, the Knicks

established themselves as one of the classiest teams in the

BAA and then in the National Basketball Association

6 (NBA), which was formed three years later. Ned Irish, the club's

founder, had a clear-cut philosophy. "We will create first-class conditions

for a first-class team in a first-class city," he declared.

Thanks to Irish, the Knicks boasted the league's first training

camp, its first athletic trainer, and its most aggressive scouting program.

Irish also found a first-class coach to lead his new squad: Joe Lapchick,

who left nearby St. John's University to take over the local pro team.

ALLAN HOUSTON

The Knicks shined in their early years behind the great play of Carl Braun.

CARL BRAUN

Lapchick's reputation as a basketball genius helped him draw top

young talent to the Knicks. In 1947, for example, Carl Braun—an out-

standing baseball and basketball prospect—decided to

break his contract with the New York Yankees just for

the chance to play basketball under Lapchick. The young

forward quickly became the Knicks' top offensive star

and was named to the NBA All-Star team five times dur-

ing his 12-year career in New York.

Braun was joined in New York by center Harry Gallatin, guards

Dick McGuire and Ernie "Doc" Vandeweghe, and forward Vince

Boryla. These players, collectively known as the "New York Five," were

small (no player stood taller than 6-foot-6) but lightning-quick, and

they played great team basketball. The New York Five reached the NBA

Finals in 1951, 1952, and 1953, but they were never quite able to bring

DICK McGUIRE

Like his father Ernie, forward Kiki Vandeweghe was a talented Knicks scorer.

KIKI VANDEWEGHE

home a championship trophy.

Then age began to slow down some of the Knicks' best players.

Starting with the 1956–57 season, New York finished last in its division 9 out of 10 years and made the playoffs just once. Talented players such as forwards Kenny Sears and Willie Naulls and guard Richie Guerin gave the Knicks some strong performances, but they never jelled to find success as a team.

Richie Guerin earned a place in Knicks history by scoring 57 points in one **1959–60** game.

{HOLZMAN BUILDS A TEAM} In 1967, Knicks management hired the perfect coach to reverse the club's losing trend: William "Red" Holzman. Holzman strongly believed that, in order for the club to return to its winning ways, individuals had to be willing to sacrifice some of their own statistics for the good of the team.

Under Holzman's direction, the Knicks drafted and traded for a

WILLIS REED

remarkable group of team-oriented players. First, there was center Willis

Reed, the club's captain and inspirational leader. The 6-foot-9 Reed was

wide and strong, and he had the heart to outfight bigger players. Joining

him in New York's frontcourt were forwards Dave DeBusschere, who

was all power and determination, and Bill Bradley, who was tireless and

had a deadly outside shot.

The team's backcourt consisted of Walt Frazier, a flashy guard who was both an offensive threat and defensive stalwart, and Dick Barnett,

The Knicks destroyed opponents in **1969–70**, winning a team-record 18 games in a row.

an outstanding clutch performer. Coming off the bench were long-range bomber Cazzie Russell and defensive specialist Phil Jackson, a gangly forward who would later become one of the NBA's most successful coaches.

Holzman molded these individuals into an outstand-

14 ing and unselfish unit. "It was a chemistry with the Knicks, a blend of individuals that resulted in communication," explained DeBusschere. "We found that when we got those lines of communication open, the willingness to sacrifice to help our team or teammates—not expecting anything in return—was a common goal."

{CHAMPIONS AT LAST} Holzman's team reached its peak in 1969–70, winning a club-record 60 games and storming through the

WALT FRAZIER

first two rounds of the playoffs. For the fourth time in their history, the

Knicks prepared to battle for an NBA title. Their opponents this time

were the Los Angeles Lakers, led by future Hall-of-Famers Wilt

Chamberlain, Jerry West, and Elgin Baylor.

The teams split the first four games, with two going into overtime.

New York won game five but lost Willis Reed when the captain tore a leg muscle driving to the basket. With Reed out, Chamberlain easily dominated game six, reducing the series to a one-game showdown.

Just before game seven began, Reed decided to play despite his painful injury. He announced the decision to his teammates, who were thrilled to have their captain back. "It was like getting your right arm sewed back on," said Cazzie Russell. The hometown fans went wild as Reed walked onto the court for the opening tip. In their hearts, the game and the championship were already won.

Forward Bill Bradley played a key role in bringing New York NBA titles in both **1970** and **1973**.

Reed scored just four points early in the game, but his presence was enough to key a Knicks victory. Of course, it didn't hurt that Frazier had the game of his life, scoring 36 points and handing out 19 assists. After 23 years, the Knickerbockers were champions at last.

Three years later, the Knicks won a second title with a slightly

BILL BRADLEY

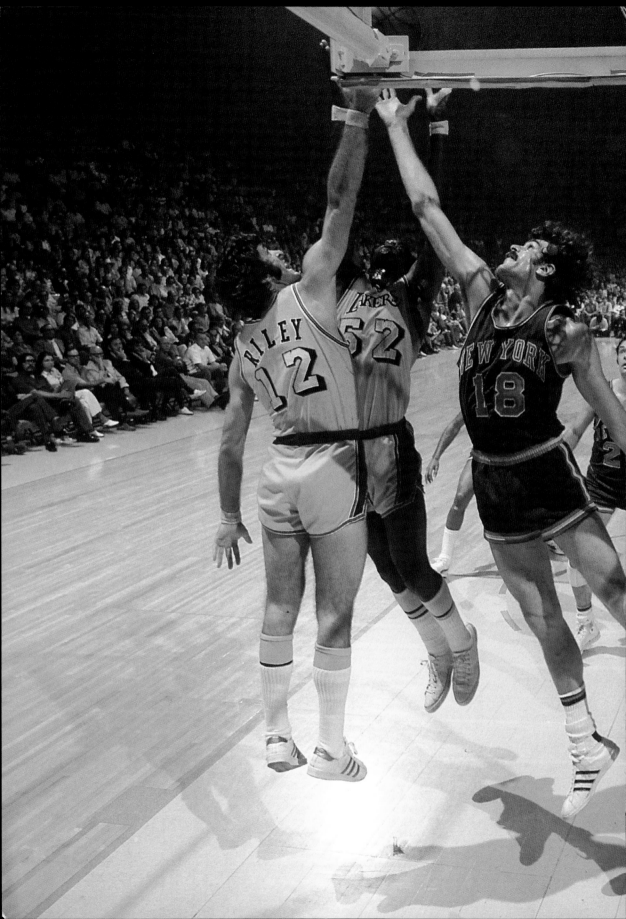

Phil Jackson, who would later gain fame as a coach, spent 10 seasons with the Knicks.

different cast. Barnett had retired and was replaced in the starting line-up by high-scoring guard Earl "the Pearl" Monroe, one of the most cre-

ative offensive players in NBA history. Backing up Reed at center was future Hall-of-Famer Jerry Lucas. The Frazier-Monroe backcourt directed another balanced New York attack and propelled the Knicks to a four-games-to-one rout of the Lakers for the 1973 championship.

{KING TAKES COMMAND} Unfortunately, Holzman's Knicks could not earn a third title. One by one, the team's core players retired or were traded away and replaced by younger stars such as guards Ray Williams and Micheal Ray Richardson and towering center Bill Cartwright. After the Knicks stumbled to a 33–49 record during the 1981–82 season, Holzman decided to retire.

Holzman was replaced by Hubie Brown, whose strict style varied

BERNARD KING

greatly from that of his predecessor. Under Coach Brown, the Knicks

ran a patterned offense and pressed and trapped on defense. It took the

players a while to adapt to this new style, but they finally succeeded.

One key reason for their success was the play of forward Bernard

King, who arrived in New York in 1982. A fierce competitor, the 6-foot-7

King could hit consistently from the outside, but his specialty was driving inside. "Bernard has an incredibly explosive first step to the bas-

ket," marveled Coach Brown. King also had the uncanny ability to get

his shot off while on the way up, before any looming

defenders could block it.

King averaged more than 26 points per game in his

first year with the Knicks and led the NBA with nearly

33 points a night the next season. Stingy defense and

Nicknamed
the "Human
Eraser," center
Marvin
Webster
rejected 131
shots in
1982–83.

22 King's scoring propelled New York to the playoffs in both 1983 and

1984. Unfortunately, the Knicks came to rely too heavily on King. When

the star forward was lost to injury early in 1984–85, the club sank

quickly in the standings.

{PATRICK BECOMES "THE FRANCHISE"} Thanks to their

low finish in 1984–85, the Knicks were awarded the top pick in the

1985 NBA Draft. With that pick, they chose a player who would be the

MARVIN WEBSTER

PATRICK EWING

heart of the team for the next 15 years—center Patrick Ewing. "The

Patrick Ewing Era Has Begun," a May 13, 1985, headline in the *New

York Times* announced.

An outstanding defender and scorer at Georgetown

University, Ewing had led the Hoyas to three NCAA Final

Four appearances, and the Knicks were counting on the

7-footer to lead them to glory as well. Ewing was a domi-

A New York native, Mark Jackson led the NBA with 10 assists a game in **1987–88**.

nant presence in the paint and boasted a deadly fadeaway jump shot. He **25**

also had a brooding "game face" that intimidated opponents.

The Ewing era in New York got off to a rocky start. It took several

years—and several coaching changes—before the Knicks were able to sur-

round their powerful center with the right supporting cast. This lineup

included point guard Mark Jackson, power forward Charles Oakley,

shooting guards John Starks and Gerald Wilkens, and forward Johnny

Newman. Together, they helped New York begin a string of playoff

appearances that started in 1988 and continued throughout the 1990s.

Before the 1991–92 season, the Knicks also added a new coach—

the legendary Pat Riley, who had guided the Lakers to four NBA cham-

pionships during the 1980s. With Riley's pushing and prodding, the

Knicks became one of the top teams in the NBA during his four years in New York. They reached the Eastern Conference Finals twice and the

NBA Finals once in search of another title.

The Knicks came closest to that goal in the 1994

playoffs, when they grabbed a three-games-to-two lead

over the Houston Rockets and needed just one more

victory to claim the crown. It never came. Cold outside

shooting, primarily by Starks, and the Knicks' failure to get

the ball inside to Ewing in the crunch led to two heartbreaking defeats.

Larry Johnson helped New York remain an Eastern Conference power in the late **'90s**.

{NEW COACH, NEW CAST} Riley left New York in 1995 to

take over as coach of the Miami Heat. He was eventually replaced by his

longtime assistant, Jeff Van Gundy. The coaching shuffle was the first

of many changes in New York. New general manager Ernie Grunfeld

engineered a major face-lift, putting forwards Larry Johnson and Buck

Williams and guards Allan Houston and Chris Childs in Knicks

LARRY JOHNSON

uniforms. Draft picks and key trades added point guard Charlie Ward, swingman Latrell Sprewell, and high-flying center Marcus Camby.

Through it all, the one consistent thread was Patrick Ewing, though injuries began to take their toll on the All-Star's effectiveness.

This new cast put together an amazing run in 1998–99. The Knicks barely made the playoffs but hit

their stride in the postseason. First, New York shocked the top-seeded Miami Heat in the first round, when a running one-hander by Houston slipped through the basket with less than a second left in the deciding game five. The Knicks wiped out Atlanta in the next round, then took on Indiana in the Eastern Conference Finals.

Things looked bleak when Ewing was lost to a season-ending injury in game two against Indiana. But the Knicks rallied—just as they

CHARLIE WARD

had in 1970 when Willis Reed went down—and beat the Pacers.

Unfortunately, New York's magical run was brought to a halt in the

NBA Finals, when the San Antonio Spurs ended the

Knicks' championship hopes.

An early exit from the playoffs in 2000 convinced

Knicks management that it was time for a major change.

In a controversial move, the Knicks decided to trade

Forward Kurt Thomas came off the bench to contribute six rebounds a game in **1999–00**.

Ewing, sending him to Seattle. Ewing's departure after 15 years in New

York was an emotional one. "Patrick is a champion, even if he hasn't

won a championship yet," said Coach Van Gundy. "He practiced and

played like a champion each day he was here."

With Ewing gone, the Knicks implemented a new offense based

on the outside shooting and inside slashing of Houston, Sprewell, and

newly acquired forward Glen Rice. Responsibility in the paint fell to

KURT THOMAS

With his long wingspan, Marcus Camby was a great rebounder and shot blocker.

MARCUS CAMBY

Latrell Sprewell used his great speed to become a deadly scorer.

LATRELL SPREWELL

Camby, power forwards Kurt Thomas and Larry Johnson, and reserve

center Luc Longley. Fans counted on this core to take New York to the

top once more.

For more than 50 years, the New York Knicks have

certainly lived up to founder Ned Irish's vision of "a first-

class team in a first-class city." Loyal New York fans have

come to expect excellent basketball in Madison Square

Garden, and that is just what today's Knicks expect to deliver.

GLEN RICE